For information, please contact:
PickYourNOsbook@gmail.com

ISBN: 979-8-9934522-0-3 Hardback
ISBN: 979-8-9934522-1-0 Paperback

1

About the Author

Inspired daily by the adventures of raising her twin daughters,
Suzanne Mercer created Pick Your NOs to equip children
and parents with confidence, empathy, and tools for everyday life.
Suzanne holds a B.S. in Psychology from University of Florida
(Go Gators!), a Doctorate in Chiropractic from Parker University,
and her Reformer certification through STOTT® pilates.
Suzanne enjoys long walks with her dog, Maui, going to the gym,
spending time with family and friends, watching trivia shows
and crime dramas with her husband, grounding at the beach,
and walking alongside her kids as they grow.
She believes health comes from the inside out, beginning with
healthy boundaries and a healthy attitude. She hopes this book inspires
readers to exercise their 'choice-making muscles,' so that with practice,
choosing kindness, protecting physical and emotional safety, and honoring
healthy boundaries becomes part of who you are.

About the Illustrator

Layla Sage Merenda is a ten year old artist living in Las Vegas, Nevada. She lives
with her sister Avery, her brother Ryder and their little black and white dog
Oreo. In her free time, she enjoys playing with Oreo, drawing and sketching!
Illustrating this children's book was an exciting and fun experience!

2

Follow Ella and Hannah, twin sisters who are full of curiosity, creativity, big feelings, and lots of energy as they explore everyday situations.
Their mom is learning to _'pick her nos'_:
setting boundaries and teaching trust
by saying yes more and
saving no for when it really matters.

There are THREE kinds of nos in this book:
- **SAFETY NO**: to keep someone safe
- **KINDNESS** or **FAIRNESS NO**: to protect someone's feelings or keep things fair.
- **SELF-CARE NO**: when a parent or kid needs to take care of themselves

First, get to know the concept of "NO."
Then test your skills.
You'll get to choose what mom says and
see how each decision plays out.
Try different paths and
talk about how each choice feels!

3

Ella and Hannah are curious kids.
They like to jump, explore,
and ask lots of questions.
One day, they heard something
new from Mom.

"I've decided," Mom said with a wink,
"I'm going to pick my NOs.".

Ella and Hannah tilted their heads and giggled.
"Pick your what?"

4

"My NOs!" said Mom.

Safe, Kind,
Fair
✓ boundaries

"If it's not
unsafe,
unkind, or
unfair
and **doesn't
cross my boundaries**...
maybe I don't need to say NO." 5

"So… can I wear this to dinner?" Asked Ella

Pajama Dress.
Leggings.
Shirt over dress.
shorts over leggings.

Mom smiled. "Yes you can! That's not a
safety, **kindness**, or **fairness** NO.
That's a you-do-you kind of YES!"

At breakfast, Hannah grabbed the orange juice. "I want to pour it myself!"

Mom paused. Was this a **'self-care'** NO?
Mom was trying to decide if she had the energy to clean up, if a big mess was made.
She quickly decided it was a learning yes.
"I know you're capable. You should try!" said Mom.

Hannah poured… and spilled a little. "Oops!"   7
Mom laughed. "Learning is messy. Still a YES."

Later, Ella and Hannah
started jumping on the couch.
"Boing! Boing!"

"That," said Mom, "is a **safety** NO.
Let's put pillows on the floor and bounce there
instead."

8

Every time Mom picked her NOs, Ella
and Hannah knew there was a reason.

When Mom said yes, they knew she believed in
them... and that what they were doing was safe
(and usually new or fun or both!).
Mom always reminds them,
"I choose my yesses and I pick my NOs,
so you can grow.".

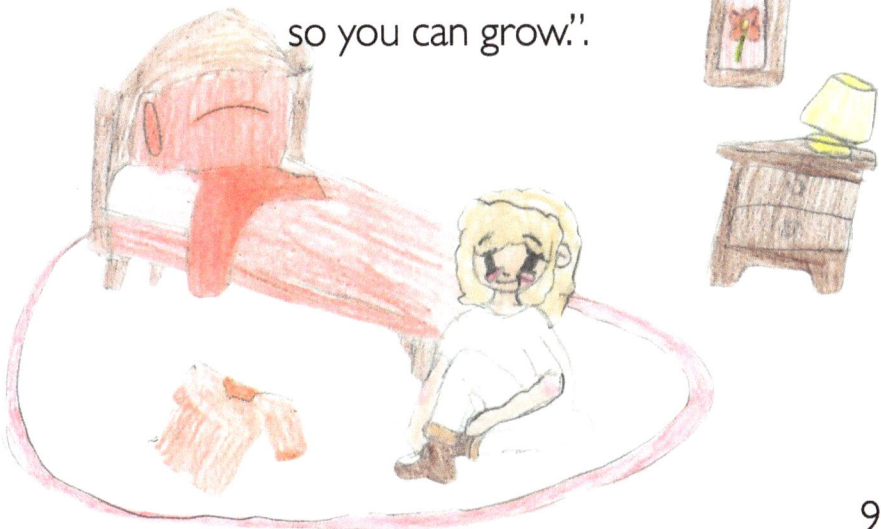

Ella and Hannah learned how to
pick their NOs, too, in all sorts of situations:
"NO, I'm not hungry
right now."

"NO, I won't share this toy, it's extra special to me.
You can borrow this one though."
"NO, I don't want a hug right now."

"I'd rather play
something else,
this doesn't feel
safe."

"No, it's not **kind** to exclude them. We can all
play together."

Mom always listened *to what they wanted.*
She didn't always say "YES."
But they always knew that what they wanted
mattered,
even if she didn't agree to it.

Ella and Hannah
still heard NOs,
but they usually
understood
the reason.

And when they heard yes?
They felt empowered. They felt trust.

11

So now, at their house, everyone
picks their NOs
and grows their yesses.

Keep going for a 'choose your path' experience...

Ella and Hannah are standing on the sidewalk.
They look across the street and see their friend's
dog wiggling happily in the front yard.
"We want to go pet him!" they say.
"No cars are coming! Can we run over?"

What should Mom do?
If Mom says YES, turn to page 14
If Mom says NO, turn to page 15

Mom lets them run ahead but, suddenly, a car turns the corner faster than expected. She yells, "Stop!" The car slows down, but everyone feels rattled. Mom says, "That was a close call. Next time, we stay together."

Turn the page to see what would have happened if mom had picked her **safety** NO.

Mom says, "It's never safe to cross the street without a grown-up. Even if it looks clear, cars can come quickly."

She takes their hands and adds, "Let's cross together ... and next time, always wait for me."

They cross safely and enjoy playing with the dog. Everyone feels protected and connected.

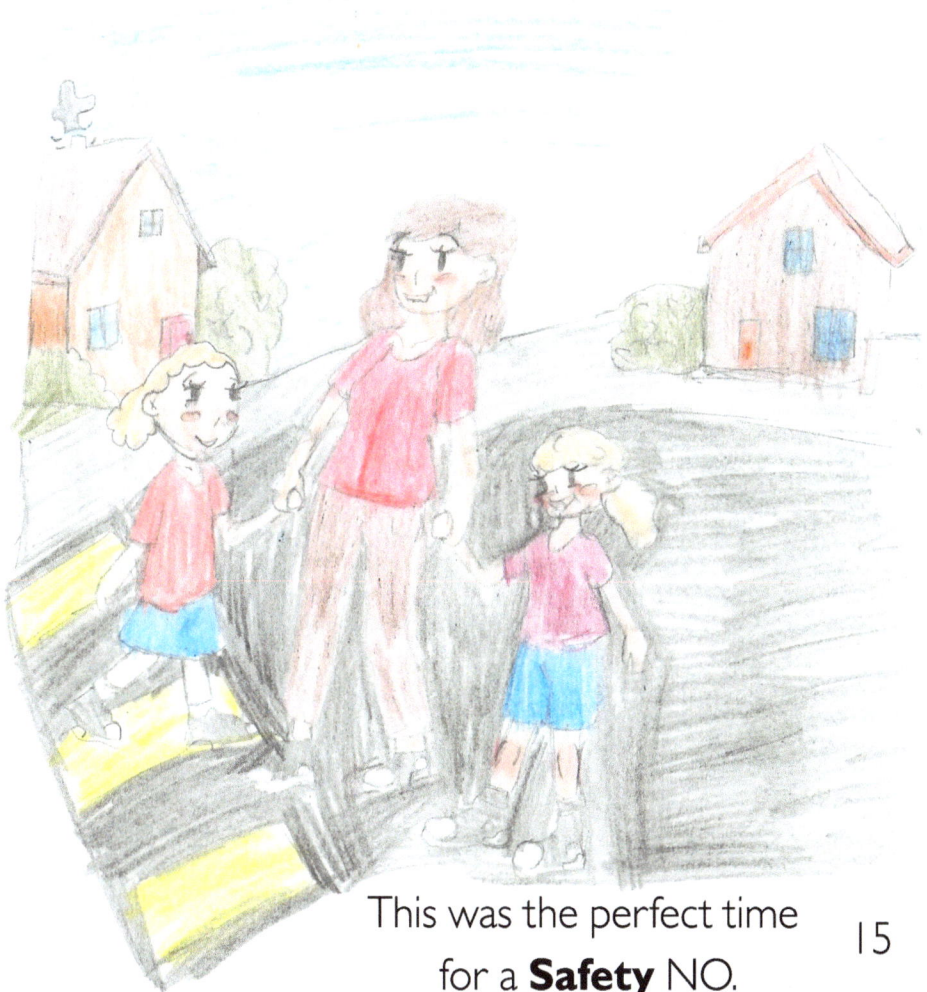

This was the perfect time for a **Safety** NO.

Ella and Hannah are feeling artsy. "We want to paint!
In the kitchen! Right now!" they shout.
Mom is cleaning and it's slippery.
She looks around at the spotless counters.

What should Mom do?
If Mom says YES, turn to page 17.
If Mom says let's think of a plan B, turn to page 19.
If Mom says NO, turn to page 20.   16

Mom says, "Okay, sure! Let's paint in the kitchen."
Paint splatters. Fingers smear colors.
The floor gets polka-dotted. The kitchen is very
messy now, but the kids are giggling and full of joy.

Later, Mom says, "That was fun, but next time
let's plan better. I need help cleaning now."

First, turn the page to help mom clean. Then, see
what would have happened if you'd chosen a
different path.
If Mom says let's think of a plan B, turn to page 19.
If Mom says NO, turn to page 20.

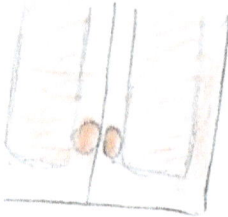

Ella and Hannah help mop,
rinse paintbrushes,
and dry the floor.

"It was worth it," Mom smiles.
"but next time, we'll paint outside."

This was a Growing Yes. Messy, but meaningful.

Mom says, "We can't paint in the kitchen right now, it's so clean. Plus, it's slippery and not safe. But I love your idea!".

She sets a timer and says, "In one hour, we'll go outside to paint together.". Ella and Hannah feel a little disappointed, but also excited to paint outside in an hour.

Turn to page 17 to see what would've happened if Mom said YES.

Turn to page 20 to see what would have happened if mom said NO.

You see what could have been:
no mess, no stress,
but also no happy giggles.

Some situations call for an alternative YES option.
We can find a compromise that keeps everyone
safe, happy, and heard! 20

Hannah says, "Mommy, I saw a cookie
in the kitchen. Can I split it with Ella?"
Mom pauses. It's not really snack time, but
that was so thoughtful.
She didn't ask for the whole cookie.
She asked to share it with her sister.
That matters.

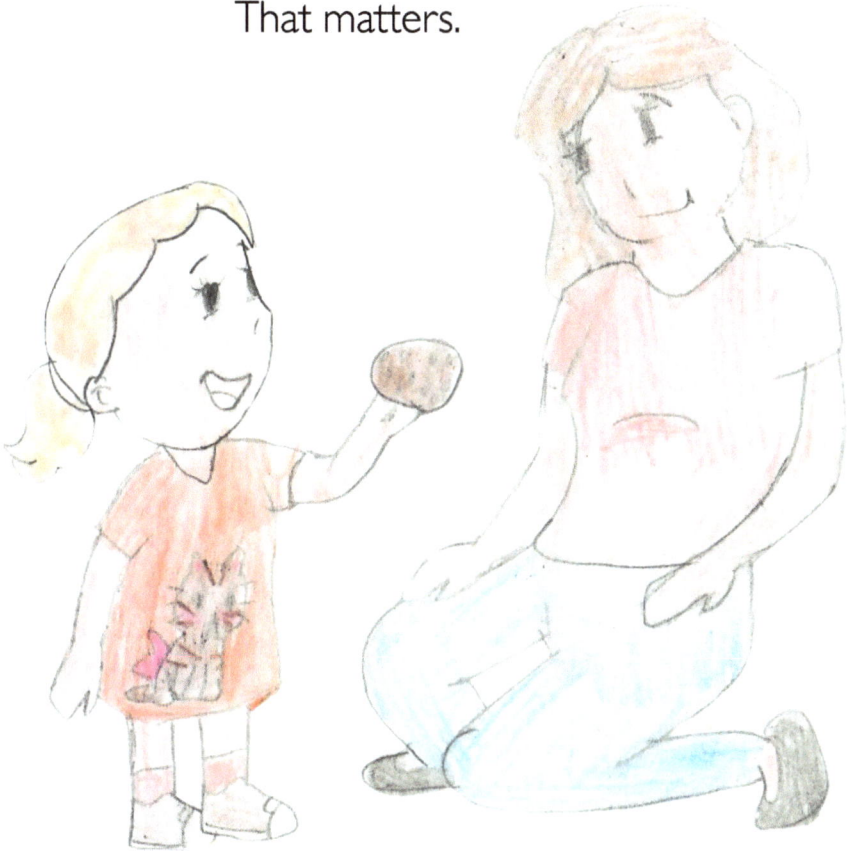

What should Mom do?
If Mom says YES, turn to page 22
If Mom says NO, turn to page 23

She kneels down and smiles gently.
"That was such a kind idea," she says.
"It's not really snack time, but the way you
asked to share it with your sister was so thoughtful.
You can split it this time, but next time let's ask
before we go looking for cookies."

Hannah smiles widely. The cookie is split.
Suddenly this small moment becomes something
bigger.

A kindness & fairness YES.
Unnecessary snack? Maybe.
A meaningful sister moment? Absolutely 22

She kneels down and smiles gently. "That was such a kind idea," she says. "It's not time for a snack. Next time let's ask before we go looking for cookies"

Hannah looks down. Her shoulders slump. Her little heart feels a little disappointed. The kind idea didn't lead to a kind moment. Even though Mom praised her, all she really remembers is no cookie, no sharing, no sister moment.

Lesson learned? Maybe. Disappointment? Definitely.
Was that choice worth it?

It's bedtime. Mom reads Ella and Hannah
one of their favorite stories. When it's done, the
girls both chant, "One more! One more!"
Mom is sleepy.
She had a very long day
and still has work to
finish.

What should Mom do?

If Mom says YES, turn to page 25
If Mom says NO turn to page 26

Mom yawns and says, "Okay, one more.". She loves Ella and Hannah SO much that it's hard to say no. It seems to take *forever* for them to agree on the last book. After reading, she's extra tired. She doesn't get her work done. She thinks to herself:

I really shouldn't have read more. I'm so tired.

The kids are happy, but Mom feels burned out.

Mom kneels beside their beds and says,
"I love reading with you, but I'm out of energy.
I need to take care of myself, too. Tomorrow night
we'll start earlier and read an extra book."

The girls grumble a little, but fall asleep feeling
loved and Mom feels good about her decision.
She set a good example.

That was a **Self-Care** NO.
That means mommy needs to take care of herself,
just like she takes care of you.

Thank you for reading **Pick Your NOs**,
I hope you enjoyed the book.
Learning to **Pick Your NOs** is an important skill
and learning to have confidence when you
hear or say YES is just as valuble.
My hope is that this book helps you choose the
right path as you travel through life's many
adventures.

Time to reflect.
Let's talk about your NOs (and YESSES):

- Can you think of a time your parent said "NO" and you understood why, even if you weren't happy about it?

- How do you feel when someone says "NO" to you?

- How do you feel when you say "NO" to someone else?

- What was your favorite "NO" in the story?

- What was your favorite "YES" in the story?

- What is a time someone said "YES" to you and how did that make you feel?

- Is there a time someone said "NO" and you think they should have said "YES"?

www.ingramcontent.com/pod-product-compliance
Lightning Source LLC
Chambersburg PA
CBHW040307070426
42447CB00029BA/36